G000077216

PRAYERS TO REMEMBER

An Essential Selection of Classic Prayers

Edited by
COLIN PODMORE

Foreword by the Bishop of London

DARTON·LONGMAN + TODD

First published in 2001
by Darton, Longman and Todd Ltd
1 Spencer Court
140–142 Wandsworth High Street
London SW18 4JJ

ISBN 0–232–52424–6

A catalogue record for this book is available from the British Library

Designed and produced by Sandie Boccacci
in QuarkXPress on an Apple PowerMac
Set in Adobe Garamond
Printed and bound in Great Britain by
The Cromwell Press, Trowbridge, Wiltshire

For Geoffrey

Contents

Foreword

Spontaneity is highly valued, but its effect on praying, both in private and in public, can be disappointing. As we search for the right words, the thinking faculty tends to predominate and interrupt the flow of communication between our spiritual heart and God. Extempore public prayer in particular requires spiritual maturity and simplicity of a high order and it can frequently degenerate into embarrassing prolixity and a lecture style of address to the Almighty.

The use of prayers learnt by heart, far from being a threat to spiritual authenticity, can be a liberation. All prayer demands relaxed attention and the use of set prayers has got a bad name in some quarters because of a failure to pray with this kind of attention. Prayers composed by some mature guide to the Way, however, and committed to memory, can reverberate creatively and powerfully in our inner spaces. The remembered prayer stands ready to enrich our understanding of fresh experiences. At the same time, the prayer we have by rote can be an undistracting yet channelling vehicle for the communication, in the Spirit of God, of sighs and groans too deep for words.

Colin Podmore has assembled a collection of prayers which are not intended to be perused by restless readers in search of novelty or fine language. These are prayers to be remembered and thoroughly digested.

Just as we are rightly careful about the quality of the food we eat, we ought to search out the finest fruits of the Christian spiritual tradition. We are indebted to Colin

Podmore for having assembled a basket of such fruits ready for us to taste and see how gracious the Lord is.

+ Richard London:

THE RT REVD RICHARD CHARTRES
Bishop of London

Introduction

This book of prayers, compiled not only for laypeople but also by a layman, has three principal aims.

First, it seeks to provide prayers which may be used by members of the congregation in private devotion before, during and after the Eucharist and other services. To these are added prayers for use at home, especially in the morning and in the evening.

Second, this book seeks to draw together prayers which are both worth remembering and easy to remember – because of their clear structures and memorable phrases. Unless people carry books with them, their only access to printed prayers during the service is to those contained in the service book or hymn book. Turning to the right prayers can be time-consuming and distracting, even if one knows where to find them; moreover, service books and hymn books do not contain the full range of devotional material, and not all churches provide them anyway. The simpler alternative is to learn some suitable prayers by heart.

Third, the book aims to gather together some of the best of prayers in English which might otherwise be lost sight of. Many of the prayers in this book were written or translated for use at Matins or especially Evensong, 'after the third collect', but full congregational services of Matins and Evensong are now held less widely than they were in the past, and where they are still offered, they are less well attended. Anglican clergy and laypeople have become more confident in praying in their own words, so simple intercessions frequently replace more formal prayers. These developments have meant that books like those from which many of these prayers are taken are no longer in print, and such prayers are less frequently heard.

A number of the prayers may be found in more comprehensive collections, but there too they may be lost sight of, among the multitude of other prayers. This is therefore deliberately a short book, and makes no attempt to be comprehensive. It does not seek to cover every possible subject for prayer, nor does it seek to include representative prayers from every period, or from various traditions. It is a personal selection, and is merely intended for laypeople who wish to extend their repertoire of memorable and remembered prayers. Many of the collects in the Book of Common Prayer and the collects and post communions in *Common Worship* are worth learning by heart, but they are relatively easy to find there. I have therefore included just a few examples in this book – one collect for each of seven principal seasons of the Christian year, seven collects which address other themes in the book, and one post communion.

At first sight, many of the prayers may not appear particularly 'relevant to the modern world'. There are plenty of books of prayers written out of and for life today, and this book does not seek in any way to compete with them. The collections from which the prayers in this book were taken are full of prayers which now, sometimes only fifty years after they were composed, seem hopelessly dated; the same fate undoubtedly awaits most, though not all, of the compositions of today which are their modern replacements. The prayers in this book are worth remembering because they have a timeless quality about them. They are in fact relevant to every age because they address themes of universal significance. Many speak of eternal life – which breaks in on the world, and is signified to it, in the Church and especially in the mystery of the Eucharist – and of the Christian way to eternal life.

Prayers are learned not only from books but also from people, and I wish to acknowledge my debt to those from whom I learned some of these prayers and devotions, including the late Canon Stuart Barrie, the Revd Professor Dennis Nineham and especially the Rt Revd Dr Geoffrey Rowell, to whom this book is dedicated. I am also indebted to my friend and sometime colleague Rachel Boulding for her invaluable advice concerning publication of the book.

Here, then, are some prayers to remember, memorable prayers worth remembering not just because of their beauty, but also because of that of which they speak. As we remember these prayers, and him to whom they are addressed, may he remember us in his kingdom.

COLIN PODMORE
All Saints' Day 2000

I: PRAYERS BEFORE WORSHIP

1. Before worship

Cleanse our consciences,
we beseech thee O Lord,
by thy visitation:
that our Lord Jesus Christ,
when he cometh,
may find in us a dwelling prepared for himself;
who liveth and reigneth with thee
in the unity of the same Spirit,
ever one God, world without end. Amen.

This prayer from the eighth-century Gelasian Sacramentary appeared in English translation in the Office of Preparation for Holy Communion in The Priest to the Altar *(1865) by P.G. Medd (1829–1908).*[1]

2. Before worship

Almighty God,
unto whom all hearts be open,
all desires known,
and from whom no secrets are hid;
Cleanse the thoughts of our hearts
by the inspiration of thy Holy Spirit,
that we may perfectly love thee,
and worthily magnify thy holy Name;
through Christ our Lord. Amen.

The Collect for Purity in the Book of Common Prayer Holy Communion service. This was translated for the 1549 Prayer Book from a prayer in the Sarum Missal which the priest said while vesting in the sacristy.

3. Before the Eucharist

Most gracious God,
incline thy merciful ears to our prayers,
and enlighten our hearts
   by the grace of thy Holy Spirit;
that we may worthily approach thy holy Mysteries,
and love thee with an everlasting love;
through Jesus Christ our Lord. Amen.

This prayer from the mass according to the Use of York was expanded from a Gallican collect of the time of Charlemagne. This translation appeared in The Priest to the Altar *(1865) by P. G. Medd.*[2]

   The prayer 'Prevent us, O Lord' (no. 45) is also suitable for use both before and after worship.

II: PRAYERS DURING THE EUCHARIST

4. During the Eucharistic Prayer

Jesu my Lord, I thee adore;
O make me love thee more and more.

This refrain from the hymn 'Jesu, my Lord, my God, my All' by Henry Collins (1827–1919) can be used as a silent response to the words 'Do this in remembrance of me'.

5. Before receiving communion

Of your mystical Supper, Son of God,
receive me today as a communicant;
for I will not tell of the Mystery to your enemies;
I will not give you a kiss like Judas;
but like the Thief I confess you:
Remember me, Lord, in your Kingdom.

In the Orthodox Liturgy of St John Chrysostom this is one of the prayers said by the clergy before receiving communion. It is also sung during the communion of the people.

6. Before receiving communion

Not unto judgment nor unto condemnation
be the partaking of thy holy mysteries to me, O Lord,
but unto the healing of my soul and body.

In the Orthodox Liturgy of St John Chrysostom this is one of the prayers said by the clergy before receiving communion. This translation was published in 1939.

7. Before receiving communion

We do not presume to come to this thy Table,
O merciful Lord,
trusting in our own righteousness,
but in thy manifold and great mercies.
We are not worthy
so much as to gather up the crumbs under thy Table.
But thou art the same Lord,
whose property is always to have mercy:
Grant us therefore, gracious Lord,
so to eat the flesh of thy dear Son Jesus Christ,
and to drink his blood,
that our sinful bodies may be made clean by his body,
and our souls washed through his most precious blood,
and that we may evermore dwell in him,
and he in us. Amen.

The Prayer of Humble Access in the Book of Common Prayer Holy Communion service. Originally composed for the 1548 Order of Communion, it reached this form in the 1552 Prayer Book.

8. Before receiving communion

Most merciful Lord,
your love compels us to come in.
Our hands were unclean,
our hearts were unprepared;
we were not fit
even to eat the crumbs from under your table.
But you, Lord, are the God of our salvation,
and share your bread with sinners.
So cleanse and feed us
with the precious body and blood of your Son,
that he may live in us and we in him;
and that we, with the whole company of Christ,
may sit and eat in your kingdom. Amen.

This alternative prayer of humble access, the work of Professor David Frost, dates from 1971. It appeared in The Alternative Service Book 1980.

9. After receiving communion

O God, who in a wonderful sacrament
hast left unto us a memorial of thy passion:
Grant us so to venerate the sacred mysteries
    of thy Body and Blood,
that we may ever perceive within ourselves
    the fruit of thy redemption,
who livest and reignest with the Father and the Holy Ghost,
ever one God, world without end. Amen.

*The Roman collect for Corpus Christi, composed by St Thomas Aquinas
(c. 1225–1274) in 1264, is addressed to God the Son. It exists in a variety of translations.*[3]

10. After receiving communion

Father of all,
we give you thanks and praise,
that when we were still far off
you met us in your Son and brought us home.
Dying and living,
he declared your love,
gave us grace,
and opened the gate of glory.
May we who share Christ's body live his risen life;
we who drink his cup bring life to others;
we whom the Spirit lights give light to the world.
Keep us firm in the hope you have set before us,
so we and all your children shall be free,
and the whole earth live to praise your name;
through Christ our Lord. Amen.

This post-communion prayer, the work of Professor David Frost, dates from 1971. It appeared in The Alternative Service Book 1980.

III: PRAYERS AFTER WORSHIP

11. After worship

Grant, O Lord,
that what we have said and sung with our lips,
we may believe in our hearts
and show forth in our lives;
for Jesus Christ's sake. Amen.

Traditional.
The prayer 'Prevent us, O Lord' (no. 45) is also suitable for use both
before and after worship.

12. After the Eucharist

God, the source of all holiness
   and giver of all good things:
may we who have shared at this table
   as strangers and pilgrims here on earth
be welcomed with all your saints
   to the heavenly feast on the day of your kingdom;
through Jesus Christ our Lord. Amen.

The post communion for All Saints' Day in Common Worship. *It comes
from* The Promise of His Glory: Services and Prayers for the Season
from All Saints to Candlemas *(1991).*

13. After the Eucharist

May the sacred feast of thy table, O Lord,
always strengthen and renew us;
guide and protect our weakness amid the storms of this world,
and bring us into the haven of eternal salvation;
through Jesus Christ our Lord. Amen.

*A prayer from the seventh-century Leonine Sacramentary, translated by
William Bright for his* Ancient Collects *(1861).*[4]

14. After the Eucharist

Finished and perfected,
so far as in us lies,
O Christ our God,
is the mystery of thy dispensation.
For we have held the remembrance of thy death,
we have seen the figure of thy resurrection,
we have been filled with thine unending life,
we have had fruition of thine inexhaustible delight,
whereof in the world to come withal
be thou pleased that we all
be accounted worthy. Amen.

This prayer from the Liturgy of St Basil was included in the Preces Privatae *of Lancelot Andrewes (1555–1626), Bishop of Winchester. The translation is by F. E. Brightman (1856–1932).*[5]

15. After the Eucharist

Strengthen, O Lord, the hands
    which have been stretched out to receive thy holy things,
that they may daily bring forth fruit to thy divine glory.
Grant that the ears which have heard thy songs
    may be closed to the voice of clamour and dispute;
that the eyes which have seen thy great love
    may also behold thy blessed hope;
that the tongues which have uttered thy praise
    may speak the truth;
that the feet which have walked in thy courts
    may walk in the region of light;
that the souls and bodies which have fed upon thy living body
    may be restored to newness of life.
And with us may thy great love for ever abide,
that we may abundantly render back praise,
praise to thy Sovereignty. Amen and Amen.

This prayer is extracted from a prayer which is said by the deacon during the communion of the people in the ancient Liturgy of Malabar, India. This version appeared in Daily Prayer, *edited by Eric Milner-White and G.W. Briggs (1941).*

IV: DEVOTIONS

16. The *Angelus*

The angel of the Lord brought tidings to Mary,
And she conceived by the Holy Ghost.

Hail Mary, full of grace, the Lord is with thee. *Luke 1:28*
Blessed art thou among women,
and blessed is the fruit of thy womb Jesus. *Luke 1:42*
Holy Mary, Mother of God,
pray for us sinners now
and at the hour of our death. Amen.

Behold the handmaid of the Lord.
Be it unto me according to thy word. *Luke 1:38*

Hail Mary ...

And the word was made flesh,
And dwelt among us. *John 1:14*

Hail Mary ...

Pray for us, O holy Mother of God:
That we may be made worthy of the promises of Christ.

We beseech thee O Lord,
pour thy grace into our hearts;
that, as we have known the incarnation of thy Son Jesus Christ
by the message of an angel,
so by his ✝ cross and passion
we may be brought unto the glory of his resurrection;
through the same Jesus Christ our Lord. Amen.

BCP collect for the Annunciation

This devotion, which originated in the later Middle Ages, recalls the centrality of the Incarnation. It is traditionally said in the early morning, at noon and in the early evening. A bell is rung three times at each 'Ave' (Hail Mary) and nine times for the collect.

17. The *Regina Coeli*

Joy to thee, O Queen of heaven, alleluia:
He whom thou wast meet to bear, alleluia,
As he promised hath arisen, alleluia,
Pour for us to him thy prayer, alleluia.

Rejoice and be glad, O Virgin Mary, alleluia.
For the Lord hath risen indeed, alleluia.

O God,
who by the resurrection of thy Son
our Lord Jesus Christ
hast given joy to the whole world:
grant we beseech thee,
that aided by the prayers of his Mother, the Virgin Mary,
we may obtain the joys of life eternal;
through the same Christ our Lord. Amen.

This devotion, dating from the twelfth century, replaces the Angelus from Easter Day until Pentecost.

18. *Anima Christi*: a eucharistic devotion

Soul of Christ, sanctify me.
Body of Christ, save me.
Blood of Christ, inebriate me.
Water from the side of Christ, wash me.
Passion of Christ, strengthen me.
O Good Jesu, hear me.
Within thy wounds hide me.
Suffer me not to be separated from thee.
From the malignant enemy defend me.
In the hour of my death call me.
And bid me come to thee.
That with thy saints I may praise thee,
For ever and ever. Amen.

This prayer, traditionally ascribed to St Ignatius Loyola (1491–1556) because it is used at the outset of his Spiritual Exercises, *is in fact very much older. It appears to date from the early fourteenth century.*

19. Thanksgiving

For the gift of his Spirit,
Blessed be Christ.

For the Catholic Church,
Blessed be Christ.

For the means of grace,
Blessed be Christ.

For the hope of glory,
Blessed be Christ.

For the triumphs of his Gospel,
Blessed be Christ.

For the lives of his saints,
Blessed be Christ.

In joy and in sorrow,
Blessed be Christ.

In life and in death,
Blessed be Christ.

Now and unto the end of the ages,
Blessed be Christ.

From 'A Thanksgiving for the Resurrection' by Eric Milner-White (1884–1963).

V: PRAYERS FOR THE SEASONS

20. Advent

Almighty God, give us grace
that we may cast away the works of darkness,
and put upon us the armour of light,
now in the time of this mortal life,
in which thy Son Jesus Christ
   came to visit us in great humility;
that in the last day,
when he shall come again in his glorious Majesty
   to judge both the quick and the dead,
we may rise to the life immortal,
through him who liveth and reigneth
   with thee and the Holy Ghost,
now and ever. Amen.

The collect for Advent I in the Book of Common Prayer, for use every day in Advent. This was composed by Thomas Cranmer (1489–1556), Archbishop of Canterbury, for the 1549 Prayer Book. It draws on two ancient Advent collects from the Gregorian and Gelasian sacramentaries, the first of which is based on Romans 13:12, a verse from the traditional epistle for Advent I.

21. Christmas

O God,
who makest us glad with the yearly remembrance
   of the birth of thy only Son, Jesus Christ:
Grant that as we joyfully receive him for our redeemer,
so we may with sure confidence behold him,
when he shall come to be our judge;
who liveth and reigneth with thee and the Holy Ghost,
one God, world without end. Amen.

The collect for Christmas Eve in the 1928 Prayer Book. It is a translation, made in 1549, of the ancient Roman collect for the vigil mass of Christmas, except that 'remembrance' is substituted for 'expectatione'. In the 1549 Prayer Book it was the collect for the first communion of Christmas.

22. Lent

Almighty and everlasting God,
who hatest nothing that thou hast made,
and dost forgive the sins of all them that are penitent;
Create and make in us new and contrite hearts,
that we worthily lamenting our sins,
and acknowledging our wretchedness,
may obtain of thee, the God of all mercy,
perfect remission and forgiveness;
through Jesus Christ our Lord. Amen.

The collect for Ash Wednesday in the Book of Common Prayer, composed for the 1549 Prayer Book. It is for use every day in Lent. It was based partly on one of the prayers for the blessing of ashes on this day.

23. Holy Week

Almighty God,
whose most dear Son went not up to joy
   but first he suffered pain,
and entered not into glory before he was crucified:
Mercifully grant that we,
walking in the way of the cross,
may find it none other than the way of life and peace;
through the same thy Son Jesus Christ our Lord. Amen.

This collect was written by William Reed Huntington (the American originator of the Chicago–Lambeth Quadrilateral) and first published in his Materia Ritualis *(1882). The first part is based on the following sentence from the exhortation in the Visitation of the Sick in the Book of Common Prayer, composed for the 1549 Prayer Book: 'For he himself went not up to joy, but first he suffered pain; he entered not into his glory before he was crucified' – a sentence which in turn was based on a quotation from Hermann of Cologne. It became the collect for the Monday of Holy Week in the American Book of Common Prayer, and was adopted as the collect for Lent III in* The Alternative Service Book 1980 *and* Common Worship.

24. Easter

Lord of all life and power,
who through the mighty resurrection of your Son
overcame the old order of sin and death
to make all things new in him:
Grant that we, being dead to sin
and alive to you in Jesus Christ,
may reign with him in glory;
to whom with you and the Holy Spirit
be praise and honour, glory and might,
now and in all eternity. Amen.

The collect for Easter Day in Common Worship. *This was the first of the two collects for Easter Day in* The Alternative Service Book 1980. *It is based on the Easter collect in* Modern Collects, *published by the Church of the Province of South Africa in 1972. The second part echoes a collect from the Gregorian Sacramentary which appeared in the Sarum* Processionale *and the 1549 and 1928 Prayer Books.*

25. Ascensiontide

Grant, we beseech thee, Almighty God,
that like as we do believe thy only-begotten Son
our Lord Jesus Christ
to have ascended into the heavens;
so we may also in heart and mind thither ascend,
and with him continually dwell,
who liveth and reigneth with thee and the Holy Ghost,
one God, world without end. Amen.

The collect for Ascension Day in the Book of Common Prayer – an
embellished translation of the ancient Roman collect from the Gregorian
Sacramentary, made for the 1549 Prayer Book.

26. Pentecost

Come Holy Spirit,
fill the hearts of your faithful people,
and kindle in them the fire of your love.

Send forth your Spirit, O Lord
And renew the face of the earth.

God, who as at this time
didst teach the hearts of thy faithful people,
by the sending to them the light of thy Holy Spirit;
Grant us by the same Spirit
to have a right judgement in all things,
and evermore to rejoice in his holy comfort;
through the merits of Christ Jesus our Saviour,
who liveth and reigneth with thee,
in the unity of the same Spirit,
one God, world without end. Amen.

The collect for Whit Sunday in the Book of Common Prayer. This trans-
lation of the ancient Roman collect for Pentecost from the Gregorian
Sacramentary was made in 1549. Omitting 'as at this time', it may be
used throughout the year.

27. Morning

O Lord, our heavenly Father,
Almighty and everlasting God,
who hast safely brought us to the beginning of this day;
Defend us in the same with thy mighty power;
and grant that this day we fall into no sin,
neither run into any kind of danger;
but that all our doings may be ordered by thy governance,
to do always that is righteous in thy sight;
through Jesus Christ our Lord. Amen.

The third collect at Morning Prayer in the Book of Common Prayer. This is a translation, made in 1549, of the ferial collect from the Sarum office of Prime.

28. A Compline collect

Visit, we beseech thee, O Lord, this place,
and drive from it all the snares of the enemy;
let thy holy angels dwell herein to preserve us in peace;
and may thy blessing be upon us evermore;
through Jesus Christ our Lord. Amen.

This prayer from the 1928 Prayer Book is translated from the Roman Breviary.

29. A Compline collect

Lighten our darkness, we beseech thee, O Lord;
and by thy great mercy defend us
    from all perils and dangers of this night;
for the love of thy only Son, our Saviour, Jesus Christ.
Amen.

The third collect at Evening Prayer in the Book of Common Prayer. This is a translation, made in 1549, of a prayer from the eighth-century Gelasian Sacramentary which was the collect in the Sarum office of Compline.

30. A Compline collect

O Lord Jesus Christ, son of the living God,
who at this evening hour didst rest in the sepulchre,
and didst thereby sanctify the grave
to be a bed of hope to thy people:
Make us so to abound in sorrow for our sins,
which were the cause of thy passion,
that when our bodies lie in the dust,
our souls may live with thee;
who livest and reignest with the Father and the Holy Ghost,
one God, world without end. Amen.

The first two lines of this prayer from the 1928 Prayer Book are drawn from a fourteenth-century Compline collect. The continuation is by Edward Willis (1844–1898), Vice-Principal of Cuddesdon College and founder of the Oxford Mission to Calcutta.

31. A Compline collect

Look down, O Lord, from thy heavenly throne,
illuminate the darkness of this night
   with thy celestial brightness,
and from the sons of light banish the deeds of darkness;
through Jesus Christ our Lord. Amen.

This prayer from the 1928 Prayer Book is translated from the eighth-century Gelasian Sacramentary.

32. A Compline collect

Be present, O merciful God,
and protect us through the silent hours of this night,
so that we who are wearied
by the changes and chances of this fleeting world,
may repose upon thy eternal changelessness;
through Jesus Christ our Lord. Amen.

This prayer from the 1928 Prayer Book is translated from the seventh-century Leonine Sacramentary.

33. For Saturday evening

As the watchmen look for the morning,
So do we look for thee, O Christ.
Come with the dawning of the day,
And make thyself known in the breaking of bread.
For thou art our God for ever and ever. Amen.

This evening prayer looks forward to the celebration of the Eucharist the next morning. It was in use in the 1960s, but its origins are obscure. The first four lines appear as versicles and responses at the end of Compline in Common Worship.[6]

34. For Sunday evening

O Lord,
who by triumphing over the powers of darkness
didst prepare our place in the new Jerusalem;
Grant us, who have this day given thanks for thy resurrection,
to praise thee in that city, whereof thou art the light;
where with the Father and the Holy Ghost
thou livest and reignest
one God, world without end. Amen.

A prayer by William Bright (1824–1901), Regius Professor of Ecclesiastical History in the University of Oxford.

35. An evening commendation

Into thy hands, O Father and Lord,
we commend this night our souls and our bodies,
our parents and homes, friends, neighbours and kindred,
our benefactors and brethren departed,
all folk rightly believing,
and all who need thy pity and protection:
light us with thy holy grace,
and suffer us never to be separated from thee,
O Lord in Trinity, God everlasting. Amen.

This prayer, adapted from a prayer of St Edmund of Abingdon (c.1180–1240), appeared in Memorials upon Several Occasions *(1933) by Eric Milner-White.*[7]

36. An evening prayer

Abide with us, O Lord,
for it is toward evening and the day is far spent.
Abide with us and with thy whole Church.
Abide with us in the evening of the day,
in the evening of life,
in the evening of the world.
Abide with us with thy grace and bounty,
with thy holy word and sacrament,
with thy comfort and blessing.
Abide with us when comes the night of affliction and fear,
the night of doubt and temptation,
the night of bitter death.
Abide with us and with all thy faithful ones, O Lord,
in time and eternity. Amen.

This prayer was written by Georg Christian Dieffenbach in 1853. A translation appeared in The Church in Germany in Prayer *(1937).*[8]

VII: PRAYERS FOR PEACE AND JUSTICE

37. For peace

O God, who art the author of peace and lover of concord,
in knowledge of whom standeth our eternal life,
whose service is perfect freedom;
Defend us thy humble servants in all assaults of our enemies;
that we, surely trusting in thy defence,
may not fear the power of any adversaries,
through the might of Jesus Christ our Lord. Amen.

The second collect at Morning Prayer in the Book of Common Prayer. In the Book of Common Prayer, the second collects at both Morning Prayer and Evening Prayer are translations of prayers in the eighth-century Gelasian Sacramentary. In the Sarum Breviary, this one is said at Matins.

38. For peace

O God, from whom all holy desires,
all good counsels,
and all just works do proceed;
Give unto thy servants that peace which the world cannot give;
that both, our hearts may be set to obey thy commandments,
and also that, by thee,
we being defended from the fear of our enemies
may pass our time in rest and quietness;
through the merits of Jesus Christ our Saviour. Amen.

The second collect at Evening Prayer in the Book of Common Prayer. In the Book of Common Prayer, the second collects at both Morning Prayer and Evening Prayer are translations of prayers in the eighth-century Gelasian Sacramentary. This one became the collect of the Sarum 'Memorial' for Peace.

39. For peace

O God, who wouldest fold both heaven and earth
    in a single peace:
Let the design of thy great love
lighten upon the waste of our wraths and sorrows;
and give peace to thy Church,
peace among nations,
peace in our dwellings,
and peace in our hearts;
through thy Son our Saviour Jesus Christ. Amen.

*This collect for peace by Eric Milner-White (1884–1963) appeared in
his* Memorials upon Several Occasions *(1933). During the First World
War, Milner-White had served as a chaplain on the Western Front.*

40. For justice and peace

Seek ye first His kingdom and His justice,
and all these things shall be added to you.
The fruit of the Spirit is love, joy, peace.

O God, the king of righteousness,
lead us, we pray, in the ways of justice and of peace;
inspire us to break down all tyranny and oppression,
to gain for everyone their due reward,
and from everyone their due service,
that each may live for all
and all may care for each,
in the name of Jesus Christ. Amen.

This prayer by William Temple (1881–1944), later Archbishop of Canterbury, appeared in A Call to Prayer (1917), *the first publication of the Life and Liberty movement, which sought self-government for the Church of England.*[9]

41. For social justice and responsibility

Eternal God,
in whose perfect realm
no sword is drawn but the sword of righteousness,
and no strength known but the strength of love:
so guide and inspire the work of those who seek your kingdom
that all your people may find their security
in that love which casts out fear
and in the fellowship revealed to us
in Jesus Christ our Saviour. Amen.

The first collect for Social Justice and Responsibility in Common Worship. *This was adapted from a prayer in* Parish Prayers *(1967), edited by Frank Colquhoun. The first four lines originated in a prayer by Eric Milner-White, published in his book* The Occasional Prayers Reconsidered *(1930), which drew on phrases from a sermon preached in 1619 by John Donne (1571/2–1631).*[10]

42. For the peace of the world

Almighty Father,
whose will is to restore all things
in your beloved Son, the king of all:
govern the hearts and minds of those in authority,
and bring the families of the nations,
divided and torn apart by the ravages of sin,
to be subject to his just and gentle rule;
who is alive and reigns with you,
in the unity of the Holy Spirit,
one God, now and for ever. Amen.

This, the collect for the Third Sunday before Advent in Common Worship, *was the second collect for the Peace of the World in* The Alternative Service Book 1980. *It was based on the former Latin collect for the Feast of Christ the King, introduced into the Roman Missal in 1925.*[11]

43. The still small voice

O God from whom we flee,
whose stillness is more terrible
than earthquake, wind, or fire,
speak to our loneliness
and challenge our despair;
that in your very absence
we may recognize your voice,
and wrapped in your presence
we may go forth to encounter the world,
in the name of Christ, Amen.

This collect by Janet Morley, inspired by 1 Kings 19:9–18 (Elijah and the still small voice), appeared in her booklet All Desires Known *(1988).*

VIII: PRAYERS FOR GUIDANCE AND FAITHFULNESS

44. For guidance

O God, forasmuch as without thee
we are not able to please thee;
Mercifully grant, that thy Holy Spirit
may in all things direct and rule our hearts;
through Jesus Christ our Lord. Amen.

The collect for Trinity XIX in the Book of Common Prayer. The collect in the 1549 Prayer Book, which was based on the ancient Roman collect from the eighth-century Gelasian sacramentary, was modified in 1662.

The prayer may be made specific by saying '... may in this and all things ...'.

The collect for Whit Sunday (no. 26), omitting 'as at this time', is also suitable.

45. For guidance

Prevent us, O Lord, in all our doings
with thy most gracious favour,
and further us with thy continual help;
that in all our works
begun, continued, and ended in thee,
we may glorify thy holy Name,
and finally by thy mercy obtain everlasting life;
through Jesus Christ our Lord. Amen.

*This prayer from the Book of Common Prayer Holy Communion service
is a translation of a prayer from the Gregorian Sacramentary. 'Prevent'
here means 'go before'. In* Common Worship *it is the post communion
for the Fourth Sunday before Lent.*

46. For faithfulness

Almighty God, in whom we live and move and have our being,
who hast made us for thyself,
so that our hearts are restless till they rest in thee:
Grant us purity of heart and strength of purpose,
that no selfish passion may hinder us from knowing thy will,
no weakness from doing it;
but that in thy light we may see light clearly,
and in thy service find our perfect freedom;
through Jesus Christ our Lord. Amen.

This prayer draws on phrases from the Confessions *of St Augustine of Hippo (354–430).*

47. For faithfulness

Remember, O Lord, what thou hast wrought in us,
and not what we deserve;
and as thou hast called us to thy service,
make us worthy of our calling;
through Jesus Christ our Lord. Amen.

This prayer from the 1928 Prayer Book is a condensed translation by Joseph Armitage Robinson (1858–1933) of a prayer from the seventh-century Leonine Sacramentary.

48. For faithfulness

O God, who art the light of the minds that know thee,
the life of the souls that love thee,
and the strength of the wills that serve thee:
Help us so to know thee that we may truly love thee,
so to love thee that we may fully serve thee,
whose service is perfect freedom;
through Jesus Christ our Lord. Amen.

This prayer is based on some phrases of St Augustine of Hippo (354–430).[12]

49. For faithfulness

Thanks be to thee, my Lord Jesus Christ:
for all the benefits which thou hast given me;
for all the pains and insults which thou hast borne for me.
O most merciful Redeemer, friend and brother:
may I know thee more clearly,
love thee more dearly,
and follow thee more nearly,
for ever and ever. Amen.

This prayer is known as the Prayer of St Richard of Chichester. St Richard (c. 1197–1253) was Bishop of Chichester from 1245. The Life of St Richard records him as having uttered the first sentence of the prayer on his deathbed. The remainder seems to have been added in the early twentienth century.[13]

50. For the presence of God

God be in my head, and in my understanding;
God be in mine eyes, and in my looking;
God be in my mouth, and in my speaking;
God be in my heart, and in my thinking;
God be at mine end, and at my departing.

A fifteenth-century English prayer, found in Sarum Primers.

51. For closeness to God

O Lord Jesus Christ,
who hast said that thou art the way, the truth, and the life:
Suffer us not at any time to stray from thee, who art the way;
nor to distrust thy promises, who art the truth;
nor to rest in any other thing than thee, who art the life;
beyond which there is nothing to be desired,
neither in heaven nor in earth;
for thy Name's sake. Amen.

This prayer consists of extracts of a translation of A Prayer to God the Son by Desiderius Erasmus (1466–1536) which appeared in A Booke of Christian Prayers *(1578). It appeared in this form in* Daily Prayer, *edited by Eric Milner-White and G.W. Briggs (1941).*[14] *Other versions replace the last three lines with various forms of the following words:*

> Teach us by thy Holy Spirit
> what to believe,
> what to do,
> and wherein to rest. Amen.

IX: PRAYERS IN THE FACE OF ETERNITY

52. To love things heavenly

Grant us, O Lord, not to mind earthly things,
but to love things heavenly;
and even now,
while we are placed among things that are passing away,
to cleave to those that shall abide;
through Jesus Christ our Lord. Amen.

A prayer from the seventh-century Leonine Sacramentary, translated by William Bright for his Ancient Collects *(1861).*

53. To lose not the things eternal

O God, the protector of all that trust in thee,
without whom nothing is strong, nothing is holy;
Increase and multiply upon us thy mercy;
that, thou being our ruler and guide,
we may so pass through things temporal,
that we finally lose not the things eternal:
Grant this, O heavenly Father,
for Jesus Christ's sake our Lord. Amen.

The collect for Trinity IV in the Book of Common Prayer is the 1549 translation of the ancient Roman collect from the Gregorian Sacramentary.

54. To be made like him

O God, whose blessed Son was manifested
that he might destroy the works of the devil,
and make us the sons of God, and heirs of eternal life:
Grant us, we beseech thee, that, having this hope,
we may purify ourselves, even as he is pure;
that, when he shall appear again with power and great glory,
we may be made like unto him
   in his eternal and glorious kingdom;
where with thee, O Father, and thee, O Holy Ghost,
he liveth and reigneth,
ever one God, world without end. Amen.

*The collect for Epiphany VI in the Book of Common Prayer was com-
posed in 1661, probably by John Cosin (1594–1672), Bishop of
Durham. It is based on 1 John 3:1–9, the Prayer Book epistle for
Epiphany VI. In* Common Worship *it is the collect for the Second
Sunday before Advent.*

55. For joy in our heavenly country

O God, who hast brought us near
    to an innumerable company of angels,
and to the spirits of just men made perfect:
Grant us during our earthly pilgrimage
    to abide in their fellowship,
and in our heavenly country to become partakers of their joy;
through Jesus Christ our Lord. Amen.

A prayer by William Bright (1824–1901).[15] *The post communion for the Fourth Sunday before Advent in* Common Worship *is based on this prayer.*

56. The house and gate of heaven

Bring us, O Lord God, at our last awakening
into the house and gate of heaven,
to enter into that gate and dwell in that house,
where there shall be no darkness nor dazzling,
   but one equal light;
no noise nor silence, but one equal music;
no fears nor hopes, but one equal possession;
no ends nor beginnings, but one equal eternity;
in the habitations of thy glory and dominion
world without end. Amen.

This prayer was composed by Eric Milner-White (1884–1963), using phrases from a sermon preached in 1628 by John Donne (1571/2–1631).[16]

57. For peace at the last

O Lord, support us all the day long of this troublous life,
until the shades lengthen, and the evening comes,
and the busy world is hushed,
the fever of life is over and our work is done.
Then, Lord, in thy mercy,
grant us safe lodging, a holy rest, and peace at the last;
through Jesus Christ our Lord. Amen.

This prayer from the 1928 Prayer Book is adapted from 'Wisdom and Innocence', a sermon preached in 1834 by John Henry Newman (1801–1890).[17]

58. To live as those who believe

O Heavenly Father,
who in thy Son Jesus Christ,
hast given us a true faith, and a sure hope:
Help us, we pray thee,
to live as those who believe and trust
    in the Communion of Saints,
the forgiveness of sins,
and the resurrection to life everlasting,
and strengthen this faith and hope in us
    all the days of our life:
through the love of thy Son,
Jesus Christ our Saviour. Amen.

This prayer appeared in the Burial Service of the 1928 Prayer Book.

59. To share the life of his divinity

Almighty God,
who wonderfully created us in your own image
and yet more wonderfully restored us
through your Son Jesus Christ:
grant that, as he came to share in our humanity,
so we may share the life of his divinity;
who is alive and reigns with you,
in the unity of the Holy Spirit,
one God, now and for ever. Amen.

The collect for the First Sunday of Christmas in Common Worship *was the first of two collects for the same day in* The Alternative Service Book 1980. *It is a translation of a collect from the seventh-century Leonine Sacramentary which was the collect for 1 January in the Sarum Missal, and is adapted from a translation made for the 1928 Prayer Book.*

X: PRAYERS FOR THE CHURCH

60. For the whole Church

O God of unchangeable power and eternal light,
look favourably on thy whole Church,
that wonderful and sacred mystery;
and, by the tranquil operation of thy perpetual providence,
carry out the work of man's salvation;
and let the whole world feel and see
that things which were cast down are being raised up,
that those which had grown old are being made new,
and that all things are returning to perfection
through him from whom they took their origin,
even through our Lord Jesus Christ. Amen.

*In the eighth-century Gelasian Sacramentary, this was the collect after
the first reading at the Easter Vigil. The translation is by William Bright
(1824–1901).*[18]

61. For the holy Catholic Church

Gracious Father,
I humbly beseech thee for thy holy Catholic Church.
Fill it with all truth;
in all truth with all peace.
Where it is corrupt, purge it;
where it is in error, direct it;
where it is superstitious, rectify it;
where anything is amiss, reform it;
where it is right, strengthen and confirm it;
where it is in want, furnish it;
where it is divided and rent asunder,
    make up the breaches of it,
O thou Holy One of Israel. Amen.

This prayer is from A Summarie of Devotions *by William Laud (1573–1645), Archbishop of Canterbury.*

62. For the peace and unity of the Church

O Lord Jesus Christ,
who didst say to thine Apostles,
Peace I leave with you, my peace I give unto you:
Regard not our sins, but the faith of thy Church,
and grant it that peace and unity which is agreeable to thy will;
who livest and reignest with the Father and the Holy Spirit,
one God, world without end. Amen.

This prayer from the 1928 Prayer Book is a translation of a collect from the Roman Missal.

63. For mission and evangelism

Almighty God,
who called your Church to witness
that you were in Christ reconciling the world to yourself:
help us to proclaim the good news of your love,
that all who hear it may be drawn to you;
through him who was lifted up on the cross,
and reigns with you
in the unity of the Holy Spirit,
one God, now and for ever. Amen.

The collect for Mission and Evangelism in Common Worship. *It was adapted from the collect for the Missionary Work of the Church in* The Alternative Service Book 1980.[19]

XI: ENDINGS

64.

May God grant
to the living grace,
to the departed rest,
to the Church and the world peace and concord
and to us sinners eternal life. Amen.

This adaptation of the Elizabethan Founder's Day prayers of Eton College and King's College, Cambridge was engraved on the west front of Westminster Abbey in 1995.

65.

Blessing and honour, thanksgiving and praise,
more than I can utter, more than I can conceive,
be unto thee, O most adorable Trinity,
Father, Son and Holy Ghost,
by all angels, all men, all creatures,
for ever and ever. Amen and Amen.

66.

To God the Father, who first loved us,
    and made us accepted in the Beloved:
To God the Son, who loved us,
    and washed us from our sins in his own blood:
To God the Holy Ghost,
    who sheds the love of God abroad in our hearts:
be all love and all glory
for time and for eternity. Amen.

By Thomas Ken (1637–1711), Bishop of Bath and Wells.

XII: GRACE BEFORE AND AFTER MEALS

67. Before meals

Be present at our table, Lord,
Be here and everywhere adored;
Thy creatures bless, and grant that we
May feast in Paradise with thee. Amen.

68. After meals

We bless thee, Lord, for this our food,
But more for Jesu's Flesh and Blood;
The Manna to our Spirits given,
The Living Bread sent down from heaven.

Praise shall our grateful lips employ,
While life and plenty we enjoy,
'Till worthy, we adore thy name,
While banqueting with Christ, the Lamb. Amen.

These verses by John Cennick (1718–1775) were included in his Sacred
Hymns for the Children of God, in the Days of their Pilgrimage *(2nd
edn, London, 1741).*

69. Before meals

Bless, O Lord, this food to our use and us to thy service;
keep us mindful of the needs of those in want,
and give us thankful hearts
for Christ's sake. Amen.

70. After meals

For these and all this mercies
may God's holy Name be praised. Amen.

Traditional.

71.

For food and friendship,
we give you thanks, O Lord.
Bless this table,
deepen our gratitude,
enlarge our sympathies,
and order our affections
    in generous and unselfish lives;
for the sake of Jesus Christ. Amen.

This prayer, supplied by Lord Runcie and adapted by Dr Ruth Etchells, is used in Church House, Westminster by Mr Colin Menzies, Secretary of the Corporation of the Church House.

72.

Praise God, from whom all blessings flow;
Praise him, all creatures here below;
Praise him above, ye heavenly host;
Praise Father, Son and Holy Ghost. Amen.

Thomas Ken (1637–1711), Bishop of Bath and Wells.

Structure of the Collects

Many of the prayers in this book are collects, and display the classical collect structure, having most, if not all, of these five elements:

- an address to God;
- a relative clause, indicating the special grounds on which we approach him;
- the petition itself (in the Prayer Book, usually beginning with a capital letter);
- the reason for or purpose of the petition;
- the conclusion.

The Collect for Purity (no. 2), for example, has all of these elements:

- Almighty God,
- unto whom all hearts be open . . .;
- Cleanse the thoughts of our hearts . . .,
- that we may perfectly love thee . . .;
- through Christ our Lord.

Textual Notes

The text of quite a few of the prayers varies from one source to another; they have been improved, adapted or simply changed in use as detailed below.

1. *Prayers in Use at Cuddesdon College* (1904) omitted the words 'thy Son' from the fourth line, and in his 1940 revision of *The Cuddesdon College Office Book*, Eric Milner-White substituted 'dwelling' for the original 'mansion'. In the original, the ending began 'Through the same Thy Son Jesus Christ our Lord, who liveth . . .'.

2. *Prayers in Use at Cuddesdon College* (1904) substituted 'approach' for the original 'minister at'.

3. This version corresponds with that printed by Percy Dearmer in *The Sanctuary* (London, 1905), except that his version reads 'Grant us, we beseech thee . . .'.

4. The words 'this' and 'eternal' were added by Eric Milner-White in his 1940 revision of *The Cuddesdon Office Book*.

5. In the original, the second line reads 'so far forth as is in our power'.

6. The prayer appears in F. Colquhoun (ed.), *Parish Prayers* (London, 1967); the author was unknown. In that version, the first line read 'As watchmen . . .' and the fourth '. . . known to us in the breaking of the bread'.

7. The text printed here follows Eric Milner-White's 1940 revision of *The Cuddesdon College Office Book* in omitting 'and servants' after 'friends'.

8. Amended versions of the translation appear in F. B. Macnutt, *The Prayer Manual* (London, 1951) and F. Colquhoun (ed.), *Parish Prayers* (London, 1967). In this version, those amendments which conform the translation more closely to the German text as printed in the *Evangelisches Gesangbuch* (no. 854) have been adopted.

9. The original has 'we pray thee' in the second line and 'for every man his' and 'from every man his' in the fourth and fifth lines.

10. Lines 1–4 are by Milner-White. Both he and Colquhoun had 'kingdom' in line 2. Line 3 is from Donne's 'Sermon of Valediction at my going into Germany', preached at Lincoln's Inn on 18 April 1619 – no. 11 of his *XXVI Sermons* (London, 1661). In the sermon, it referred not to the kingdom of heaven but to England, 'this Kingdom of peace, where no sword is drawn but the sword of Justice'. Lines 5–9 retain the structure and some of the words of Colquhoun's prayer ('for the peace of the world'), but it is considerably abbreviated, modernised and amended to widen its focus.

11. In *The Alternative Service Book 1980* the collect ended 'who is alive and reigns with you and the Holy Spirit . . .' (as did the collect for the First Sunday of Christmas – no. 59). It also served as the collect for Pentecost 15, and the collect was adapted to fit the theme for that Sunday – those in authority. The line 'govern the hearts and minds of those in authority' was added and *suavissimo* was translated 'just and gentle'.

12. There are a number of different versions of this prayer. Here, that in J. Bowden (ed.), *By Heart. A Lifetime Companion* (London, 1984) has been followed, except in the third line, where 'seek' is replaced by 'serve', which appears in other versions and accords better with the logic of the prayer.

13. The first sentence is to be found in Ralph Bocking's V*ita Sancti Ricardi auctore Radulfo* (British Library: Sloane MS 1772, f. 25). The earliest known source for the second sentence is G. R. Bullock-Webster, *Churchman's Prayer Manual* (privately published; London, 1913 [copy in the Library of York Minster]). This information is derived from M. Stone, *The Prayer of St Richard of Chichester* (privately published; 2nd edn, Chichester, 1990). The ending 'for ever and ever, Amen' was added by Eric Milner-White in *Memorials upon Several Occasions* (1933).

14. The relevant extracts from the original prayer are as follows: 'O Lord Jesus Christ . . . which hast said, that thou art the way, the truth and the life . . . I beseech thee . . . suffer me not at any time

to stray from thee, which art the way ... nor to distrust thy promises, which art the truth ... nor to rest in any other thing than thee, which are the way, beyond which is nothing to be desired, neither in heaven nor in earth ... Thou hast taught us thoroughly what to believe, what to do, what to hope, and wherein to rest ...'

15. In *Memorials upon Several Occasions* (1933), Eric Milner-White added the words 'earthly' and 'heavenly'.

16. The sermon, no. 15 in *XXVI Sermons* (London, 1661), was preached at Whitehall on 29 February 1627/8. The relevant extract is as follows: 'They shall awake as Jacob said, and say as Jacob said ... *this is no other but the house of God, and the gate of heaven*, And into that they shall enter, and in that house they shall dwell, where there be no Cloud nor Sun, no darknesse nor dazling, but one equal light, no noyse nor silence, but one equal musick, no fears nor hopes, but one equal possession, no foes nor friends, but one equal communion and Identity, no ends nor beginnings, but one equal eternity.'

17. The words 'of this troublous life' are not in the original.

18. The original read 'that things ..., that things ..., and all things ...'.

19. In *The Alternative Service Book 1980* the fourth line read 'help us so to ...', the fifth line had 'reconciled' instead of 'drawn', and the collect ended 'through him who died for us and rose again and reigns with you and the Holy Spirit ...'.

Modern-language Versions

Some of the older prayers in this book also appear, with varying degrees of adaptation, in a modern-language version in *Common Worship: Services and Prayers for the Church of England* (*CW*) or *Common Worship: Pastoral Services* (*CW:PS*). The volumes and page numbers for those modern-language versions are given here, so that those who prefer may learn them in that form.

Acknowledgements

Every effort has been made to trace and contact copyright holders. If there are any inadvertent omissions we apologise to those concerned and undertake to include suitable acknowledgements in future editions.

* indicates that a prayer has been modified.

Extracts from *The Book of Common Prayer*, the rights in which are vested in the Crown, are reproduced by permission of the Crown's Patentee, Cambridge University Press (2, 7, 16, 20, 22, 25, 26, 27, 29, 37, 38, 45, 53, 54).

Prayers taken from *The Prayer Book as Proposed in 1928* are copyright © The Archbishops' Council and are reproduced by permission (21, 29, 30, 31, 32, 47, 57, 58, 62).

Prayers from *Common Worship: Services and Prayers for the Church of England* are copyright © The Archbishops' Council, 2000 and are reproduced by permission (8, 10, 12, 24, 41, 42, 59, 63).

The prayer adapted from Archbishop William Temple (1881–1944) – most recently published in A. Wilkinson and C. Cocksworth (eds), *An Anglican Companion. Words from the Heart of Faith* (London, 1996) – is included by permission of SPCK (40*).

'Not unto judgment ...', from *The Orthodox Liturgy, being the Divine Liturgy of S. John Chrysostom and S. Basil the Great according to the Use of the Church of Russia* (London, 1939), is reproduced by permission of the Fellowship of St Alban and St Sergius (6).

Prayers from E. Milner-White and B.T.D. Smith (eds), *Cambridge Offices and Orisons* (London, 1921) (19); W. Kagerah and R.A.S. Martineau, *The Church in Germany in Prayer* (London and Oxford, 1937) (36*); and E. Milner-White (ed.), *After the Third Collect* (4th edn, London, 1952) (35, 39, 56*) are included by permission of

Mowbray Publishing, an imprint of The Continuum International Publishing Group.

Prayers from *The Divine Liturgy of our Father among the Saints John Chrysostom* (Oxford, 1995), copyright © The Greek Orthodox Archdiocese of Thyateira and Great Britain, 1995 (5), and E. Milner-White and G.W. Briggs (eds), *Daily Prayer* (London, 1941) (15, 51) are included by permission of Oxford University Press.

'O God from whom we flee ...' excerpted from *All Desires Known*, expanded edition, copyright © 1988, 1992 Janet Morley. Reprinted by permission of SPCK and of Morehouse Publishing, Harrisburg, Pennsylvania (43).

The compiler is grateful to the Very Revd Archimandrite Ephrem Lash for directing him to the source of no. 6, to Canon J. Robert Wright for information about no. 23, to Canon Roger Greenacre and the Revd Michael Stone for information about no. 49, to Mr Colin Menzies for information about, and permission to include, no. 71, and to Mr David Hebblethwaite for directing him to sources of information about some of the collects.

Other Sources

The following prayers are believed to be out of copyright. The source from which they have been taken is indicated below.

* indicates that a prayer has been modified.

67, 68: John Cennick, *Sacred Hymns for the Children of God, in the Days of their Pilgrimage* (2nd edn, London, 1741).

61: *The Works of William Laud*, ed. J. Bliss (Library of Anglo-Catholic Theology), vol. 3 (Oxford, 1853).

13, 34, 52, 55*, 60*: W. Bright, *Ancient Collects and Other Prayers* [first edition published in 1861] (5th edn: Oxford and London, 1875; facsimile: Cincinnati, 1993).

1*, 3*: [P.G. Medd], *The Priest to the Altar, or Aids to the Devout Celebration of Holy Communion, chiefly after the ancient English Use of Sarum* (London, 1865).

14: *The Preces Privatae of Lancelot Andrewes, Bishop of Winchester*, ed. F. E. Brightman (London, 1903).

65, 66: W.H. Frere and A.L. Illingworth, *Sursum Corda. A Handbook of Intercession and Thanksgiving* (2nd edn, London and Oxford, 1905).

9*: P. Dearmer, *The Sanctuary* (London, 1905).

23, 49: E. Milner-White (ed.), *After the Third Collect* (4th edn, London, 1952).

46, 48*: J. Bowden (ed.), *By Heart. A Lifetime Companion* (London, 1984).

4, 50, 72: *The New English Hymnal* (Norwich, 1986).

Further Bibliography

Books of prayers

Prayers in Use at Cuddesdon College (Oxford, 1904).

E. Milner-White, *The Occasional Prayers Reconsidered* (1930).

[E. Milner-White (ed.)], *Memorials upon Several Occasions. Prayers and Thanksgivings for use in Public Worship* (London and Oxford, 1933).

F. B. Macnutt, *A War Primer, Containing Prayers, Old and New, for Public and Private Use in Time of War* (London, 1939).

A. S. T. Fisher, *An Anthology of Prayers* (5th edn, London, 1950).

E. Milner-White, *A Procession of Passion Prayers* (London, 1951).

F. B. Macnutt, *The Prayer Manual* (London, 1951).

[E. Milner-White (ed.)], *Prayers in Use at Cuddesdon College* (London, 1961).

A Manual of Catholic Devotion for members of the Church of England (7th edn, London, 1969).

The Promise of His Glory: Services and Prayers for the Season from All Saints to Candlemas (London, 1991).

A. Wilkinson and C. Cocksworth (eds), *An Anglican Companion. Words from the Heart of Faith* (London, 1995).

Other works

F. L. Cross and E. A. Livingstone (eds), *The Oxford Dictionary of the Christian Church* (3rd edn, Oxford, 1997).

The Sermons of John Donne, ed. G. R. Porter and E.M. Simpson, vols ii, viii (Berkeley and Los Angeles, 1955, 1956).

R. C. D. Jasper and P. F. Bradshaw, *A Companion to the Alternative Service Book* (London, 1986).

A. Leak, 'Eric Milner-White's Prayers', *Friends of York Minster Annual Report* (1984), 18–23.

M. Stone, *The Prayer of St Richard of Chichester* (privately published; 2nd edn, Chichester, 1990).

M. R. Dudley, *The Collect in Anglican Liturgy. Texts and Sources 1549–1989* (Alcuin Club Collection 72, 1994).

P. Bradshaw (ed.), *A Companion to Common Worship*, vol. 1 (Alcuin Club Collection 78, 2001).